AF492303

Ultimate Sex Positions For Couples 2020

The Unique Guide For Young And Advanced Couples To Discover Ultimate Sex Positions To Revitalize Their Sex Life With Maximum Satisfaction In Marriage.

By

Derek White

Legal notice

The content of this book was written after deep research and practical experience conducted by the author.
If in any case, the content written therein does not work for you, it means you did not implement and practice exactly what was written here.
Also, if you find any grammatical and typographical errors in this book, note that it was a mistake.
Therefore, don't bend on spotting out errors, focus on learning new sexual positions to improve your marriage, and bring more joy in your family.

Copyright ©2020 Derek White
All rights reserved.

No part of this book may be duplicated, transmitted or distributed in any form or by any means, including photocopying, recording, and other mechanical or electronic methods, without the prior written permission of the publisher and the author, except in the case of brief quotations embodied in reviews and other non-commercial uses permitted by copyright law.

Dedication

This Book is dedicated to Almighty God who enabled me and gave me the inspirations to compile the solutions related to people's problems in sex life.

Table of Content

Acknowledgment

I want to commend my beautiful wife who stood by me to make this Book successful.

Introduction

The Essentials Of Sex For Couples

Sex is a beautiful thing that unites couples together emotionally, intimately, and happy to live as one. Its uniqueness has made it to be vital in marriage institution and carries the act of recreation in life.

Statistically, it has been recorded that its health benefits are enormous which is not limited to the creation of euphoria amongst couples when depression is found in their midst.

When sex is not properly practiced within couples, it tends to bring in misunderstanding and conflict which if not taken care of, might eventually lead to breakup (divorce).

Research has it that about 50% of divorce amongst couples worldwide does not emanate as a result of financial instability or religious belief but as a result of negligence given to sex within married people. This is the reason why prior attention should be given to sex in marriage to avoid problems.

In marriage, some men have high libido for sex and some women cannot pass a day without making love with her husband. As a result of this issue, due explanation has been made on two factors that you need to understand to help you and your partner to study each other and agree on the proper ways to improve on your sex life which is compatibility and intimacy.

Furthermore, there are ten benefits you will drive from sex as a Couple;

i.   Sexual intercourse relieves headaches. When you make love often, it releases the tension in the veins of the brain.

ii.   Making love always helps to clear a stuffy nose. It is a natural antihistamine. Sex helps to spring up allergies and fight against asthma.

iii.   Having sex smoothly, slowly and in a relaxed manner reduces the chances of suffering skin rashes, acne, and dermatitis. The sweat generated during lovemaking, makes your skin glow and cleanses the pores on your body.

iv.   It has been discovered scientifically that when a woman makes love, it produces a large amount of estrogen that softens the hair and makes it shine properly.

v.   Sex tends to burn all the calories you have accrued so far.

vi.   Having sex strengthens the muscles of the female and male bodies. One of the best sporting activities is embedded in sex. It is more preferable and enjoyable than swimming 50 laps in the pool and to take it a step further, you don't need a boot for this.

vii.   Frequent sex releases more pheromones.

viii.   Sexual intercourse serves as a remedy for depression. Furthermore, it releases endorphins into the bloodstream thereby creating a state of excitement and happiness.

ix.   Kissing is an act which makes the saliva and teeth to reduce the amount of acid that causes tooth decay. This is the reason why kissing daily tends to keep you away from the dentist.

x.   Sex is a muscle relaxant and tranquilizer to a safer world. It is more than valium.

xi.   Practicing a stereotyped sex life makes it boring and you wouldn't want that in your marriage.

Therefore, in this book, you shall be exposed to uncommon ultimate sex positions to practice in your marriage to revitalize your sex life to the next level.

You will also discover various ways you can reach orgasm with your partner and enjoy sex like never before.

I have also taken time to demystify foreplay and its importance, various sex positions to adopt to get pregnant and secrets to conceive a baby girl and also a baby boy during sexual intercourse.

So, I want to specially thank you for purchasing this book. I know there are thousands of books related to this topic out there but your decision to buy my book, makes me happy and I am highly grateful.

As you read through this book, you shall find solutions to what you seek.

See you on the inside!!!

Chapter one

Compatibility

The role which compatibility plays in a relationship and marriage in everyday life for couples is enormous and can never be undermined. Understanding compatibility in marriage or a relationship is vital. When it is not checkmated, it leads to misunderstanding between couples.

What is Compatibility?
The lexicon meaning of compatibility is the state of being compatible; in which two or more things can exist or work together in combination without problems or conflict.

When we narrow it down to relationship and marriage, it means a state of mutual understanding existing between two partners notwithstanding their flaws but agreed to live, stay, and work together in love and sincerity of heart.

You have seen that no man can be naturally compatible with each other. It takes meticulous effort to build a compatible relationship with someone whom you admire so much to marry.

Therefore, as you continue reading, you will understand the role of compatibility in marriage, and while it's paramount in your sex life.

Key factors in Relationship that triggers Compatibility
You have seen from the previous explanation given above that for two partners to be compatible relationship-wise, there must be trust, acceptance, and mutual understanding existing between them.

Spiritual Compatibility
Emotional Compatibility
Monetary Compatibility
Physical Compatibility
Future Compatibility

Spiritual Compatibility:
This is very paramount for couples. It is the bedrock of marriage. To achieve greater heights in life and your marriage, it is pertinent to build a strong spiritual foundation with your partner. Once you and your partner are spiritually compatible, there is no limit to what you both can achieve in life. It does not only have a positive effect on you and your wife but also to your kids and unborn kids.

Therefore, in all you do, ensure to build Spiritual Compatibility first.

Emotional Compatibility:
This is one of the key factors in a relationship that is if not checkmated, leads to a sudden breakup. It has been ascertained that women are emotional beings and must be given attention. When attention is given, trust is established and when trust is built, emotional compatibility is achieved.

Everybody on this planet earth has one flaw or the other. There is no perfect person in life. This makes us understand that there is no perfect marriage or couples if you don't build one. The euphoria single ladies and guys exude in dating cannot keep or build a long-lasting marriage.

Therefore, when you take your time to study the character of your partner both good and bad, it will enable you to know how to tolerate each other in marriage.

If your partner is sanguine and you happen to be combining phlegmatic and choleric temperament, you have to learn how to manage her temperament to suit you and also teach the other things you want her to learn and make her unlearn the ones you don't want her to keep as a wife. These corrections should be done in love to avoid misunderstanding. Once it's implemented and it's fine with her, you have finally created *emotional compatibility* with her.

Also know that you cannot achieve full compatibility during a relationship. This is because you are not living with her yet in your home. So there are some things which you think you know about her that will change in marriage. This can also be done to your husband as a wife to order to create a conducive and enjoyable home.

Monetary Compatibility:
This is an aspect that should be given serious attention. If you and your wife does not know how to manage money together, it will lead to a serious issue in the future. Therefore, you should teach your wife how to manage money and save and likewise you. This will build trust amongst both of you and prevent future misunderstanding in your marriage.

Physical Compatibility:
Physical compatibility is achieved when there is a mutual understanding between you and your partner sexually.

Let's take for instance if your husband loves making love twice a day, but you don't like doing so, it will create a state of physical incompatibility between both of you. But when you both sit down and discuss it in love, and you happen to see reasons with him why he loves making love twice a day, and later you agreed on making love with him irrespective of your principles, it will bring about physical compatibility in your sex life. All you need to do is to choose some days for sex instead of daily.

Future Compatibility:
This is a serious concern between couples. This is what depicts what both of you want in your marriage, like the number of kids you want, landed properties to acquire, vacations, and so on. Therefore, it is pertinent to agree

on your goals which you both want to achieve in your marriage and work towards it.

Now that you have been able to understand what compatibility entails in your marriage, this leads us to the section where you will discover the impact the role of intimacy in your sex life can create.

See you there!

Chapter Two

Intimacy

Intimacy plays a vital role in relationships and marriage. When it is in view, long-lasting marriage is built and it is achieved, it is, in turn, brings about a healthy sex life among couples. However, when it is not in view, there will be a catastrophe and misunderstanding amongst married people.

At first, the euphoria of falling in love before marriage has a strong force which many couples think will sustain them in marriage but in due time, it gradually fades away. This is where compatibility sets in. Now, to build a strong intimacy in marriage, you and your wife will need to work on your compatibility which I believe you must have understood in the previous chapter.

In as much as you want to learn different unique sex positions, you can practice in your home, but if your intimacy level is not checkmated, it might prove abortive.

This is the very reason I made it a point of duty to enlighten you on the importance of intimacy in your marriage so that you will enjoy the rest of what you will learn in this book.

What is Intimacy?
This is an atmosphere of oneness, openness, and trust towards someone you love which might not necessarily involve sex at the initial point.

Therefore, in the quest to build intimacy, the primary factor should be trust, openness, and oneness. When these factors are not considered, sexuality will not materialize.

There are different forms of Intimacy
Spiritual Intimacy
Emotional Intimacy
Intellectual Intimacy

Spiritual Intimacy:
The relevance of Spiritual Intimacy cannot be overemphasized. It is the bedrock of long-lasting marriage. This kind of Intimacy is built when you engage in prayers and supplications always with your partner. Conduct morning devotions together. Go to church together. When the Spirit is mutual, there is no room for what both of you can achieve in life.

This will make both of you practice any kind of sex position comfortably because physical closeness has been at the initial stage.

Emotional Intimacy:
This is a state of physical closeness, oneness, and trust. Emotional Intimacy is a form of Intimacy that requires openness to one another without hiding anything. In this form of Intimacy, Couples are meant to share their stories both past and present, even their flaws, happiness, joy, sorrows, challenges, both the ones you think you cannot mention to your wife.

Once oneness is built, it ignites trust which drives the ladder of a successful marriage.

Couples who understand the importance of emotional Intimacy hardly divide. It rather strengthens the marriage bond day by day.

Intellectual Intimacy:
This is the moment when you and your wife share and discuss probably what you learned from reading books, movies, and other things of life.

You have learned that Intimacy brings oneness and trust and thereby strengthens your sex life

See you in the section!!

Chapter Three

Practical Steps To Undertake To Prepare Your Body And Mind For Lovemaking

The following steps should be followed maintained by couples before the commencement of sexual intercourse and foreplay.

Shave your private part:
Some people don't see shaving their private part as something important. But this is one of the vital things to do before engaging in sexual intercourse. So, ensure to always shave properly so that you will not be taken unaware by your wife or your husband to make love.

Shave your armpits:
To ensure proper cleaning, also make it a point of duty to always shave your armpits. It also helps to prevent body odor.

Mouthwash:

Always brush your teeth before sex to avoid mouth odor during kissing.

Extra panties:

Ensure to always travel with extra panties. It will help you to change immediately you feel any discharge in the private part during unplanned foreplay.

Taking bath:

As a couple, it is pertinent to take your bath before sexual activities so that you both will be fresh.

Peeing:

As a woman, you don't want to be uncomfortable during sexual intercourse so that you will not terminate the already highly sexual connection built already. So make sure to always urinate before making love. This is very important not only for the wife but also for the man. As a man, if your bladder is filled up while making love, it will take you to ejaculate easily. This is what you will not like.

Farting: During lovemaking, always be conscious not to fart. This might spoil the euphoria.

You have learned all the steps to follow to be ready for sexual intercourse in this chapter.

In the next chapter, you will learn how to spice your sex life with foreplay.

See you there!!

Chapter four

Demystifying Foreplay In Sex For Couples

The role of foreplay in a relationship and marriage cannot be overemphasized. Its importance creates room for mutual understanding and triggers emotional Intimacy amongst couples.

The reason why some marriage sexual life suffers and lack of adventurous events are that foreplay must have been neglected or is not well practiced amongst them.

It is a bond that binds couples together. It makes a man to be attracted to his wife always. It makes a man love and cherishes his lady.

Have you been brainstorming on the various ways to improve your sex life, make her to always be happy and drive everlasting joy in your marriage?

Have you been thinking of the reason why your sex life has been boring for some time, especially after the birth of your dear son or daughter?

The answer to the genesis of your problem lies here. Therefore, the very reason why your sex life has been suffering is because of the lack of pre-intercourse. The importance of foreplay in your marriage and relationship cannot be underrated because it has a strong role to play in taking your sex life to the next level.

Research has it that about 20% of broken marriages worldwide are not due to financial incapability but due to non-satisfactions in their sex life.

Now, what does foreplay mean? Foreplay is a physical activity practiced between two couples before lovemaking. As the keyword sounds, it's a playful act that triggers your emotions, stimulates your genitals for sexual intercourse.

The Importance of Foreplay in your Sex Life.
Foreplay activates your physiological responses for lovemaking.

It triggers your physical responses and creates a special love bond between couples.

It stimulates your genital parts for sexual intercourse.

It rekindles an impaired love in couples.

It creates mutual understanding and strengthens your love life.

It is a form of indoor exercise for couples.

It prepares your body and mind to perform more than 30 minutes in bed with your partner naturally.

It triggers and intensifies orgasm in women.

Health Benefits of Foreplay
Engaging in foreplay activities has some health benefits attached to it.

During foreplay, kissing each other releases some chemicals like serotonin, oxytocin, and dopamine which boosts feelings and affections. It also reduces your stress hormone level in the body.

During foreplay, it causes the erection of your nipples and makes your breast to swell.

It triggers the dilation of your blood vessels.

It improves the rate of your blood pressure.

The rate of your heart is increased as well during foreplay which is good for your body.
Foreplay creates an avenue for the penis, labia, and clitoris to swell as a result of the rapid inflow of blood into your genitals.

With foreplay in view, you don't need physical lubricants to make love with your partner because immediately the sensitive parts of your partner are charged, it causes her to reach orgasm which makes the vagina to be wet for easy penetration of your penis.

Foreplay Areas that Stimulates Her to Action

Nipple Touch: Research has it that every woman has a particularly sensitive part that triggers her emotions and turns her on for lovemaking. Nipple touching happens to be one of the erogenous zones that stimulate a lady for sexual intercourse. When you are done undressing her romantically, gradually feel the breast before moving to the nipple area. Don't rub the nipple too fast. Ensure easy and relaxed touching for like 2 to 4 minutes. It will trigger her physiologically.

Nipple Sucking: Gentle sucking of the nipples can triple her sexual sensation after you might have finished touching it gradually. It is an act that will take the stimulation to the next level. All you have to do is to start sucking the nipples gently and continue licking it with the tip of your tongue for a period of 2 to 3 minutes. This act will make her wet.

Kissing: This is a unique connection that can stimulate the genitals of your partner and charge both of you to stay bonded and propels each other for sexual intercourse. The health benefit of this reduces the stress hormone of both partners. Therefore it should not be neglected during sexual intercourse.

Neck Licking: Neck licking happens to be one of the foreplay you should practice to make your sexual life improve. It is one of the sensitive parts in a woman's body that triggers her emotional intimacy to have sex. To get started, allow her to lay on the chair or bed. Gradually lick the neck region romantically. This can be done after kissing her.

Fingering of the V-Spot: Vagina fingering is an awesome act that turns her on and makes her feel you deeply even when you are yet to insert your penis into her vagina. Don't rush it. If you forcefully insert your finger into her vagina, you might injure her which can lead to serious complications. So, ensure you put at most two of your fingers into her pussy slowly. Let the activity be slow and steady, it will surely make her be excited and love you more.

Licking of Vagina: This is another pleasant pre-intercourse act which does not only engage the partner for sex but also makes her feel on top of the world because it stimulates both the vaginal and clitoral orgasm depending on how good you are to take her to reach that level. It is also known as going down on a woman.

How to get started: Ensure she clean up very well before the foreplay activity. Slowly spread her legs and gradually lick the clitoris with the tip of your tongue. The licking process should last for 5 minutes. During the 5 minutes, it will make her genitals to swell. Sucking of the vagina should commence after the licking process. Ensure deep sucking of the pussy which will make her release sexual talks for you and it will bring about a high stimulation of the clitoris. Now, she will be begging for the sex because she is fully lubricated and ready to go for many rounds with different sex positions which will be discussed in the later chapters of this book.

Sucking and Licking of Toes: This might sound awkward to you, but it is one of the sensitive areas that stimulate a woman for sex. All you have to do is to ensure that her legs are properly washed. Lick and suck mostly the first toe. It tends to send a physiological response to her emotional gland thereby activating her for lovemaking.

Licking and Biting of Butt: This is another awesome foreplay activity. Start by romancing her butts with your fingers gradually. Take it further by licking it and enhance it with some gentle bites. It will surely make her feel excited and turn her on.

Licking Anus: Licking the anus of your lady happens to be one of the proven ways to get her aroused. It increases her appetite for sex mightily. Though some couples might not find this method very fascinating. But if it's what you can do, ensure to give it a try. You might love it.

How to get started, start licking the anus slow and steady as she kneels on the bed with her hands serving as the support. You can take it a step further by squeezing her breast and rubbing the nipples altogether.

Communication in Foreplay: During foreplay, communication is one of the vital tools that stimulate sexual activity. Dirty talks like "you are hot", "hot pussy" and "give it to me baby" make the sex to be romantic.

Foreplay Tips Capable of Driving Him Crazy

Foreplay was not created to stimulate the female partner alone for sexual intercourse. It has a strong role to play on the side of the male partner as well, to achieve equilibrium and attend sexual climax.

Therefore will be discussing some pre-intercourse activities capable of driving your man crazy and prepare him to perform more than an hour with you in bed.

Contour Display:

One of the ways to make your man feel crazy about you and to remind him how sexy you look is to always undress before him. Before you undress, ensure he is sitting before you. Gently remove your trouser (anything you are wearing) while slightly bending down and backing him as well to see the lines of your underpants with your butt.

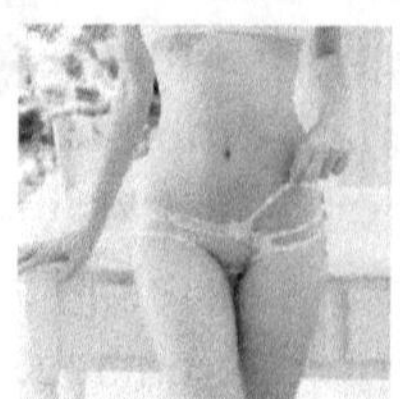

Turn around and face him. Slowly unbutton your blouse such that he will see your cleavage slowly down to your abdomen. Remove your bra gradually to allow your breast to slowly relax on your body. This will be done with a sexy look continually to his face. When you practice it often, you will surely get him aroused sexually.

Groove Display:

This is another beautiful way to express your love for him and get something in return. Your work here is to stage him on a dance. Look for one of the best songs that captivate his heart very well, turn up the volume, pull him out to the dancing floor, allow him to hold your waist, dance alongside him, and ensure your hips touch his P-spot. Dance romantically with him. It will surely get him excited and express his ultimate love for you.

Give Him Romantic Bath:

As couples, it is vital to always have your bath together. When bathing with him, try to caress him romantically with the soap from his shoulder to his chest, down to his manhood. It will make him feel loved and exude some element of joy.

Blow Job:

Make your man be aroused by giving him a blow job. Don't wait until he asks for it. Sometimes, you need to take control by luring him to the bedroom, slowly take off his clothes, kneel, hold his erected penis, caress it very well and give him a deep sucking of his life capable of driving him crazy. Though some ladies do not like performing this. But whatever your reasons are, it is essential to give your man a blow job, not once, not twice but all the time. This will make him have sex with you immediately.

Sexy Wears:

One of the best ways to always look sexy and get your man aroused towards you all the time is dressing sexy at home. What you put on matters at home. The very reason some men don't find their wives attractive anymore is not looking sexy and not checking on what you wear at home. There is no way you should be found inside your kitchen putting on a long gown. There is no way you should engage in house chaws putting wrapper.

Ensure to always wear sexually attractive clothes like bump shot, gowns that will be above your knees. Men are attracted by what they see. Don't say he has been seeing you. You have to ensure he stays loved and focused on you. It will make him not look another. It will make him to always think about you and make love to you always.

Caressing His Chest:

Some hairy guys love it when their lady caresses the hair on their chest. It arouses their emotions and also creates room for intimacy thereby leading to sexual intercourse.

Distract Him With Kiss:

The emotional Intimacy of your husband to you will spike each time you surprise him with a kiss. Make it a point of duty to kiss him before leaving the house. It makes him to always have you in the mind even while in the office. It should not just anyhow kiss. Let the kiss be unique such that it will be remarkable to him.

Immediately he comes back, don't just welcome him with a warm hug, argument it with a French kiss that will trigger him to carry out sexual activities that are capable of making you reach orgasm and thereby make love with you after he must have taken his bath and take his dinner.

Movie Play:

While watching a movie together, lay your head on his shoulder, periodically take your hand beneath his private part and squeeze it for some time. Do this periodically as the movie is going on, it will turn him on to visit the other room.

Give Him A Clean Shave:
Make it a point of duty to shave his private part and armpit once it is bushy. Men love it when their wives do this. It stimulates their emotions for sex.

Licking of Chest:
You can shift his state of equilibrium emotionally by licking his chest gradually and steadily. It makes him feel excited, happy, lovely, and erotic.

See you in the next section!!

Chapter Five

Understanding The Essentials Of Orgasm

What Is Orgasm?

According to the Cambridge lexicon, orgasm is the moment of greatest pleasure and excitement in sexual activity.

Wikiwand also states that orgasm is the sudden discharge of accumulated sexual excitement during the sexual response cycle, resulting in rhythmic muscular contractions in the pelvic region characterized by sexual pleasure.

In my understanding, orgasm is the ability to achieve maximum satisfaction during sexual intercourse which results in the discharge of fluids between the male and female partners.

Types of Orgasm
There are two classes of Orgasm, the male and the female. We will demystify the female Orgasm.

Types of Female Orgasm…

Combo Orgasm:
Combo Orgasm occurs when the clitoris and the G-spot stimulate at the same time resulting in a more intensifying Orgasm.

Anal Orgasm:
During anal Orgasm, you might feel like you want to urinate but the contractions will not be felt around the genital area.

Vaginal Orgasm: This kind of Orgasm is achieved when there is deep penetration with your partner. This makes the vaginal walls to pause.

Clitoral Orgasm:
They are felt on the surface of the body. It is like a tingly feeling along your skin and in your brain. For some ladies, having their clitoris stimulated during foreplay is capable of sending them into Orgasm.

Erogenous Zones:
These are some sensitive parts of your body which when romanced can result in Orgasm. Examples include Nipples, Neck, Ears, Elbow, Breast, Lips, Toe, and so on.

G-Spot:
This is a type of Orgasm which allows you to reach vaginal Orgasm. So, if you can be able to locate the G-spot, you have attained the intended vaginal Orgasm at the same time.

Oral Orgasm:
You can make her reach Orgasm if you can play very well with your tongue around her clitoris. It is popularly known as going down on a

woman. Believe me, this is one of the best ways to achieve multiple Orgasms with her.

Now, I know you are excited already about what you learned about Orgasm and what it can do to make your sex pleasant.

Don't wait to practice what you have learned here immediately.

See you in the next section as I deepen how mind to understand the role of tantric sex and how it will propel your sex life.

Chapter Six

Understanding Tantric Sex For Couples

Tantric sex has been in existence for more than 5000 years according to research. It is said to be an ancient sex practice that originated from Hinduism. Tantric sex happens to promote **deep intimacy and expansion of energy.** Unlike western sex practice, tantric is a slow form of sex that does not need to be rushed. Its gradual activities make it to increase intense stimulation and sensation for couples.

Why Should Couples try Tantric Sex?

If you prolong the effort, energy, and time you invest in sex, you will surely attend a new high level of intimacy and intense orgasm says, tantric professionals.

If you have been looking for strategic ways to rekindle your sex life, tantric sex should be given a try.

If you want to build a strong and irresistible bond with your partner, tantric should be in view.

The only way to reunite with your wife or husband, give tantric a try.

How to Prepare Your Mind And Body for Tantric Sex

Below are some tips you have to follow to get started with tantric sex.

Start by shutting down every other activity on your to-do-list for maximum concentration.

Bed Isolation: This kind of sex cannot be practiced on your bed to avoid sleep. This is because it requires gradual, slow, and steady activity which might last for hours.
Therefore to achieve what tantric sex offers, you must give is time.

Tantric Sex Positions for Couples

Create a Vacation Plan:
To get started with tantric sex, you need to make out time to travel to an isolated place with your partner. Shutdown every activity you have in your to-do-list. In your current location, ensure to turn off your gadgets and beautify the room with colorful flowers. Furthermore, get yourself purified by putting on something lovely after taking your bath.

Soul Gazing:

This is one of the powerful practices during tantric sex because it triggers strong intimacy. To achieve this, sit on a pillow or the ground with your partner and face each other. Both of you should hold your hands together, look up straight into each other's eyes without blinking for about 3 to 5 minutes. You are allowed to blink every 5 minutes intervals.

In the process of gazing into each other's eyes, try to feel the illumination on your partner's eyes, the force of attraction, and the sensation of love emanating from the eyes of your partner. This beautiful and awesome moment generating some sparks of love which you have not imagined since you met your partner. Practice it for like 10 minutes to 20 minutes with full concentration, you will surely discover a high level of emotional sensation you have never felt before with your partner.

Massage in Tantric:

Tantric massage is one of its kind. It is capable of driving multiple orgasms with intense stimulation. It is not the type that can be rushed at all. However, in tantric massage, one partner should lay on the ground. It can be the male or the female at first.

Begin to caress her from the shoulder down to the entire body slowly. As the process is ongoing, she will feel you, the connection will be very strong such that it will open up every sensational part in her thereby increasing the sexual energy and pleasure of tantric sex.

Also, ensure to concentrate more on the erogenous zones on her body. This process is known as yoni massage because is a tantric massage for the clitoris and vagina.

Secondly, allow the male partner to lay on the ground and perform the same massage procedures which the partner did on you. This process is also known as lingam massage. Moreover, you can as well extend the tantric massage to the next level by licking and sucking the nipples of the female partner gradually which is known as nipple play.

Hands-on Heart Contact:

This is an extension of soul gazing. Unlike the soul gazing which involved sitting on a pillow or chair with your partner facing each other with direct eye contact to express the illumination of love emanating from your heart, you need to place your hand on the heart of your partner and allow her to do the same. Try to breathe in slowly and breathe out as well.

As you breathe in, you are directly sending love signals from your heart through your hand to her heart and as she breathes out, she will send her love signals from her heart to your own heart. This process will bring about love, energy, and intimacy between both of you.

Ensure it is done more than 5 times.

Now, you have learned sex positions in a tantric way which its goal is not only targeted to *reach orgasm but to achieve a strong bond between couples and build ultimate intimacy capable of bringing forth close connection, long-lasting orgasms, multiple orgasms and high state of emotions naturally* without forcing it.

Probably tantric sex happens to be a mystery to you as well before now, but from the content, you read here, you have seen that it plays a vital role in your sex life and strengthens intimacy in marriage.

See you in the next section!!

5 Sex Positions For Beginners

Sex is a beautiful thing that bonds husband and wife together and thereby builds up strong emotional intimacy for both parties. When it is neglected in a relationship like marriage, it causes serious catastrophe which can lead to broken homes if care is not taken.

Therefore, it is pertinent to improve your sexual life occasionally. This brings us to the discussion on different uncommon sexual positions to adopt to rekindle your sex life and drive ultimate happiness with your partner.

In this section, we shall discuss the 5 sex positions for young couples who are just starting married life.

Missionary Position:
This is the simplest sexual position you can practice as a newbie in marriage as seen in the picture below.

How to get started- After you must have charged your partner up with foreplay as we discussed in chapter four, let your wife lay on the bed with her back. Spread her legs at an angle of 60 degrees for easy penetration. Insert your penis gradually inside her vagina which is already lubricated during pre-intercourse.

Ensure your two legs are in between her own. You can use your two hands as support or your elbow as a support on the bed while moving up and down inside her clitoris. Do not rush it at the initial stage, so that you will not ejaculate so fast. After about 5 minutes of gradual performance, you can take it a step further by holding her firmly for deep penetration which tends to make her make sexual noise.

If you want to spice this very position, to make it not to be boring as people see it to be, try to kiss her, suck her nipples, lick her neck as the sexual intercourse is ongoing. This will surely make her reach orgasm if you practice what has been explained here very well.

Legs Up Missionary:

This is taking the missionary position to the next level.

How to get started- In legs up missionary, immediately your wife lay on the bed, instead of spreading her legs to an angle of 60 degrees, you will lift her two legs a little. Tell her to sustain the two legs in the air as seen in the picture above. When you insert your penis into her vagina, your thighs can also serve as support to the legs so that she will not be tired too quickly while keeping the legs in the air.

Therefore, the difference between missionary and legs up missionary is that, in the former, her legs are kept on the bed flat while in the latter, her legs were suspended in the air for deeper penetration.

Reclining Lotus Position:

In this sex position, repeat the same steps discussed in legs up missionary.

The difference is that you will use a pillow to support or raise your wife's hips to be at an angle of inclination as represented pictorially above. This very position is highly suitable for men with a short penis because it will make your penis not to pull out uncontrollably. It will also enhance more penetration thereby creating sexual sensation between your wife and you.

Doggy Position:

This is another pleasurable position you can practice but it is a little technical. It is not as easy as the previously discussed positions. Also, you might not be able to feel her erogenous areas completely like the previous sexual styles.

How to get started- In this position, allow your wife to kneel on the bed and place hands on the bed as well. Her abdomen might or might touch the bed while her buttocks will be raised to an inclined angle as seen in the picture above.

The benefit of the doggy position is the extra penetration given while making love. You can be squeezing her breast as well if you can maintain the balance.

Standing Position:

You might be thinking like a beginner how to enjoy sex standing up. But it is one of the ways you can spice your lovemaking to avoid making it to be bored with constantly practicing one style.

How to get started- It is simple, allows your wife to stand and lean on a wall probably in your bedroom or in your parlor as the case may be. Let her buttocks point outwards a little and insert your penis to her vagina. While the process is ongoing, you can place your hands on her hands in the same position she placed it on the wall for more intimacy. If you don't get it well at first, do not give up. Keep on practicing until perfection is achieved as seen in the picture above.

When you are done practicing the five sex positions discussed in this chapter very well as a beginner, you can graduate to the next level.

Therefore, in the next section, we shall be discussing the ultimate sex positions strictly for advanced couples.

So, ensure to practice the beginner's sex positions here to be able to play around with the advanced sex positions.

See you in the next chapter!!!

Chapter Eight

Ultimate Sex Positions For Advanced Couples.

Best Sex Positions To Last Longer In Bed

Spooning Position:
As the name sounds, it is performed by lying side by side to each other in the bed, ground, or chair. It tends to create multiple orgasms easily. It is also a unique sex style that can be practiced in and out of season.

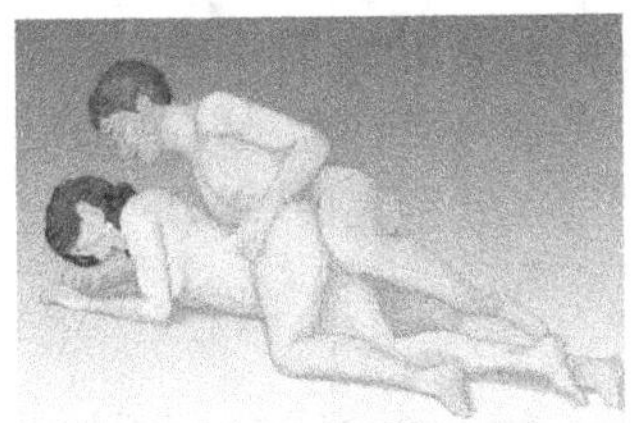

How to get started- In spooning position, allow her to lay by her side on the bed with her thighs together. Lying at her back, insert your penis from her backside by gently raising one of her butts for easy penetration. Once you are inside of her, begin to thrust. There is room for a continuation of foreplay within the erogenous zones at your reach.

One of the disadvantages is the inability to look straight into her eyes as the intercourse is ongoing. It is a long-lasting sex position because it gives room to periodical performance. The clitoral orgasm is sure with the spooning method. All you need is to allow gradual performance to avoid easy ejaculation.

Cowgirl (Her On Top):

This is a system of sexual intercourse was the wife assumes full control of the performance until a climax is achieved as seen in the picture below. Some men don't fancy it because they want their wife to be the one pumping but you can't underestimate the power of a woman during lovemaking because there is a special energy and sexual drive that controls them to the extent that some women don't get satisfied until an hour or two is reached.

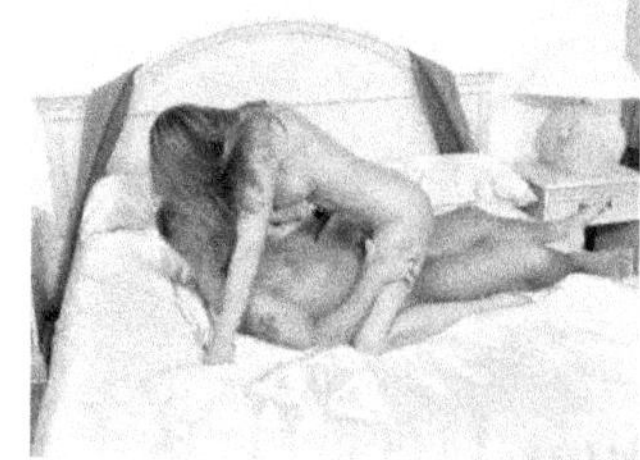

How to get started- All you have to do as the man is to gently lay on the bed flat. You can use your pillow to support your head if you wish. Hold your penis in a definite position for easy penetration into her vagina. She can also help herself by inserting the penis into her clitoris gradually. This process can last more than 2 hours for some reason. Ejaculation occurs easily when the penis is in a downward position. But in this case, the penis is in an upward position and when slow and steady movement is considered at the initial stage, it will send the spermatozoa back. When this happens, it brings about an intense feeling and excitement which on the other hand generates vaginal and clitoral orgasms.

Excited to know about this right? Enjoy!!

The Lotus Position:

This is yet another sexual position also known as cuddle squat because it allows couples to cuddle each other so well which brings about intimacy. It is essential because there is a medium for foreplay while the intercourse progresses.

How to get started- In lotus position, you are to sit down and slightly spread your legs with your penis charge already for work. Your wife is expected to sit on your erected penis and straddle her legs around your waist as she begins to make up and down movement against your penis for pleasurable sexual intercourse.

Intense orgasm and sexual satisfaction are expected in this method due to extra penetration which will be achieved. You can go on and on without getting tired because both of you are actually at work.

Koala Position:
This is another position that is highly technical but can be achieved by big sexual players if you are the type that likes carrying your wife around, this method is definitely for you. Have you imagined surprising her in the kitchen or the sitting room with hot sex unknown to her?
I guess your answer is as good as, I must give it a try.

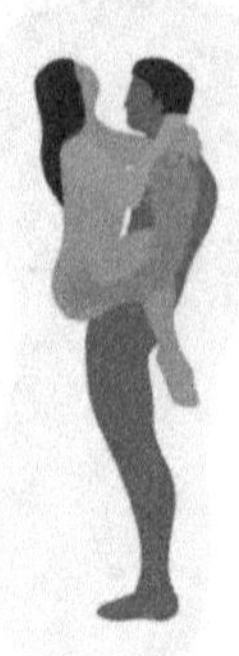

How to get started- Let's assume she is sitting in the parlor seeing a movie, probably a romantic one, your instinct should tell you that she must be probably wet at that moment. When you enter the parlor, try to tease her at first which will make her smile and play alongside you, the next thing should be a surprising lifting. Then gently give her a warm French kiss which will trigger her sensual response. Pull her underwear gradually and carry her up closer to your waist region.

The penetration of your erected penis will be easy as she holds you on your neck region firmly. Begin to perform while she is looking straight into your eyes with a deep smile.

At first, it may be difficult but continual practice will make it to be easier as time goes on. If you feel uncomfortable, you can keep her butts at the edge of your dining table and continue enjoying the beautiful moment to the fullest.

The Spider Position:
This sex position is kind of tricky and technical but it's awesome if you can try it with your wife.

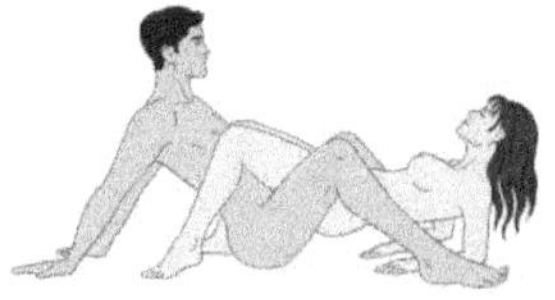

How to get started- All you have to do is, sit back with your legs spread out while resting with your hands as a pivot point. Let your wife sit back as well with her legs spread out widely for smooth penetration of your dick.

Her hands will also serve as support while she moves up and down against your dick. Your thighs and her own will be making contact as the process is ongoing.

Other Sex Positions You Can Play Around With Partner

Butter Churner Position:
In this hot sexual position, your wife should lay on her back on the floor with her legs stretched out to touch her head in the form of an alphabet "C". Then you are to squat very close to her widely open vagina. Insert your erected penis and begin to dig it gradually. This method is slightly difficult but you can give it a try. See the pictorial representation below.

Reverse Cowgirl Position:
As the name sounds, this is typically the opposite of cowgirl. In this hot sex position, you are meant to lay flat with your back on the ground or the bed depending on your choice. She will sit on your erected penis without facing you in the opposite direction as seen in the picture below.

How to get started- Also, your thighs will serve as a support for her to be able to perform effectively. One of the disadvantages of this very position is the inability to caress her erogenous zones.

The Socket Position:

This very position is not only hot but the best of is kind. It is surely a must to try sex position which can be practiced by all couples. Though it might be slightly difficult at the initial stage as time goes on, perfection must be achieved.

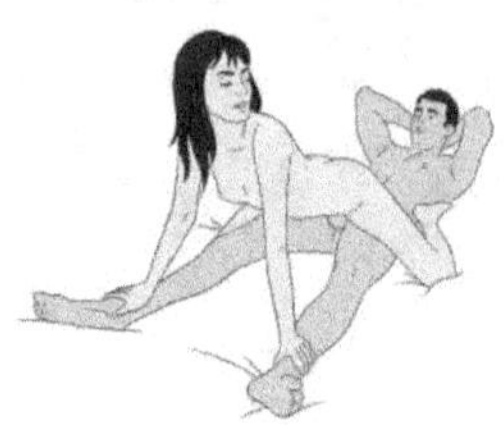

How to get started- In this sex position, you are to lay with your back on the bed or the floor with your erected penis while your spouse mounts on you with her head in the opposite direction to your own. That means her head will be pointing towards your legs while her butt will be towards your head as she penetrates.

Now, she will hold her two hands on your feet as a pivot point to enable easy movement of the vagina against your penis.

As the sexual activity is going on, you will be able to view the dangling of her butts which triples the sexual urge for you.

Reverse Socket Position:

In this position, let your wife lay on her back and spread her legs a little. Mount on her and insert your penis into her vagina in a kneeling position, then lay down as well with your head in the opposite direction to her own. The stroking will be difficult initially but the balance will be maintained afterward.

Best Positions For Penis Length.

Tominagi (Small Penis):
Allow your female partner to lay on her back with a pillow as support. Then kneel in her front and bend her legs towards her body such that her feet will be touching your chest. This very method will enable maximum satisfaction and deep penetration of your penis inside her clitoris. Don't spread her legs away from the body to ensure tight and firm to and fro movement of your penis.

Standing Doggy Style (Average Penis):
To achieve satisfactory and pleasurable lovemaking with an average penis, standing doggy position is what you need to try.
How to get started- All you need to do is to ask your partner to kneel at the edge of the bed with her hand placed on the bed as support. You will stand on the floor, hold her hips for firm movement of your penis. You don't need to wind your waist. All you need to do is to move her waist with your hands for easy to and fro movement. It makes you be in control and allows absolute deep penetration.

The Thigh Straddle (Large Penis):
Unlike the short and average penis, you need to make use of this unique method to achieve deep penetration. Therefore all you need to do is to get your legs crossed while sitting down. Then position your penis for easy penetration as you let her sit on your laps.

Sex Positions To Help Her Climax Quicker
Nirvana:
A mind-blowing and fascinating orgasm will be achieved when she lay flat on your bed with her hands stretched out and her legs tightly crossed. Then gently lay on her abdomen with your legs stretched outside and carefully insert your penis into her hot pussy and grind it slowly. An hour performance is a guarantee with a nirvana position if you practice it very well.

The Shard:
Allow her to lay on the bed. Lift her two legs and allow her ankles to find support on your shoulders with her thighs tightened very well. This will trigger her quick orgasm and make your lovemaking sweet.

Thigh Master:
Make her scream on top of her voice with this mind-blowing sex position.

How to get started- All you have to do is to lay, using a pillowcase to support your back. Straighten your right leg and fold the left one a little bit up. Let her straddle her right leg as she sits on your abdomen. Allow her to be in control as she performs with reverse cowgirl using your knee as a pivot point.

Sex Positions To Give Her Multiple Orgasms.

Sit And Straddle:
This is one of the prettiest ways to attain multiple orgasms with your partner.

How to get started- All you have to do is, find a conducive place with a sitting position, probably on your couch or at the edge of your bed. Let her jump on you and straddle you firmly. Give her full control to ride as you intensify the process by touching her breast, nipples, and kissing her while laying backward slightly.

Sideways Scissors:
This position requires both of you to lay perpendicular to one another as seen in the picture below. She will lay flat while you will be sitting with your left hand serving as support. Let her left leg cross in between your two legs while you hold her right leg with your right hand close to your waist for deep penetration as you ride slowly.

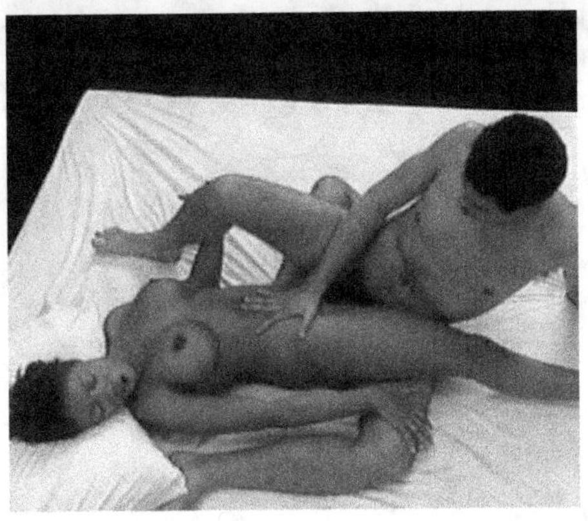

This position does not only result in deep penetration, but it also generates ultimate orgasms multiple times with intense stimulation of the clitoris.

The Table:
This method is rare and not commonly practiced by couples. But if you want to take your sex life to the next level, you need to give it a shot.

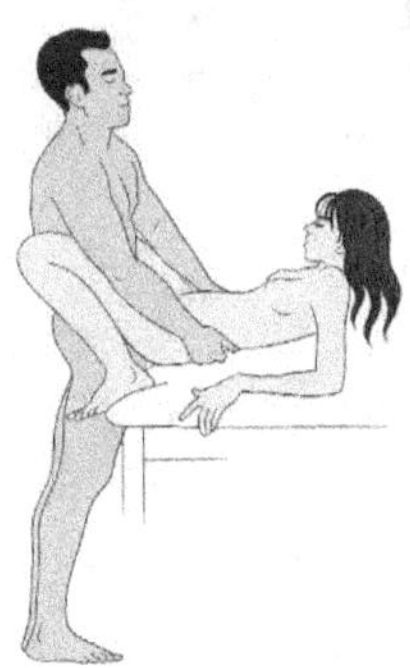

How to get started- All you have to do is to mount your partner on a table that is above your waist. Let her lay on it and stretch her legs. Insert your penis inside her pussy and thrust. She will be fired up to the extent that her clitoris will be stimulated with multiple upon multiple orgasms which will make her scream your name an uncountable number of times.

Joystick Joyride:
Sit and spread your legs a little while she sits on your laps, placing her legs on your shoulder while her hands serve as support as she rides. See the pictorial representation below.

The Sensual Spoon:

This is the advanced level of spooning position. All you have to do is to lay side by side as usual and penetrate from the back. But in this case, she will have to raise her top leg for direct and in-depth erroneous penetration with resultant multiple orgasms and satisfaction.

Advanced Hacks- Positions to Take Your Sex Life to the Next Level
The Sphinx:

This is one of the unique positions you can practice with your partner. It is beneficial to both beginners and advanced couples.

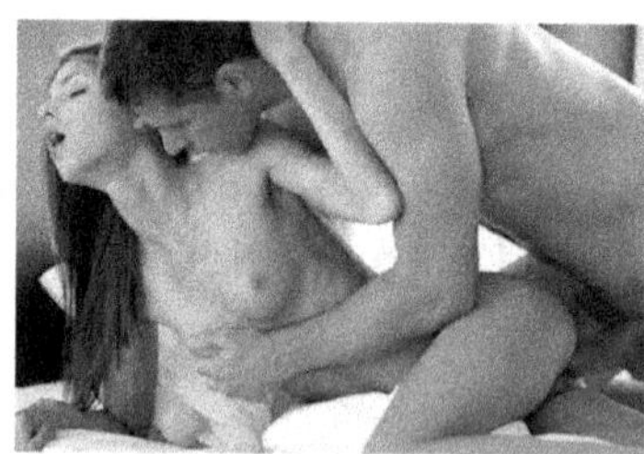

How to get started- It requires your wife to lay on the bed sideways with her face facing up to enable eye contact with each other. Stretch her left leg up to enable you to insert your penis gradually inside her pussy.

The Pretzel:

This position is pretty simple and enjoyable. What she needs to do is to kneel, lay on her left side, and straddle her left leg.

Pile Driver Position:

This is a dramatic sex position that can only be practiced by young couples.

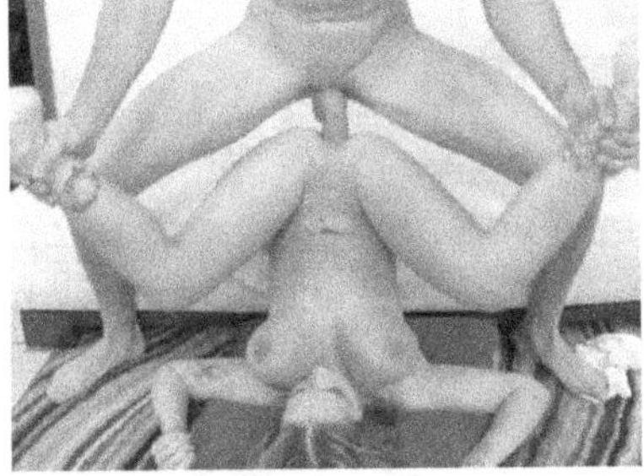

How to get started- Your wife will lay on the ground, probably in your parlor. She will rest her back on the couch. You will stand in a squatting position with your erected position to be inserted into her vagina. You will hold her legs as a support to ride properly.

Helicopter Position:

This is another adventurous position meant for young couples to explore.

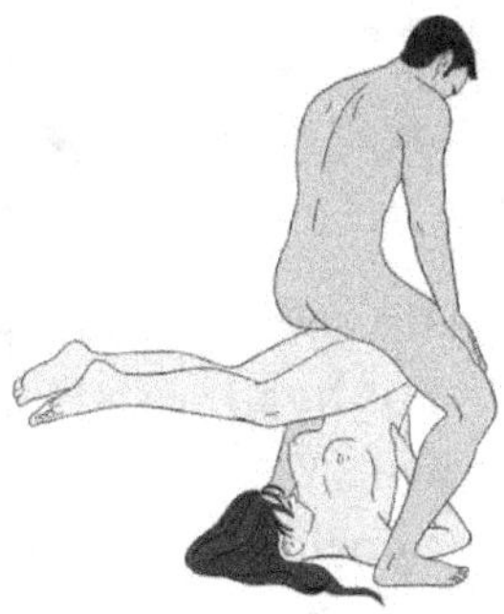

How to get started- Let your wife lay in the same position explained previously in the pile driver style. In this position, you won't be holding her two legs. You will mount on her in the opposite direction to ride properly.

The CEO Position:

This is a simple sexual intercourse position that can be practiced by young couples and old couples as well.

How to get started- Once you are done with foreplay with your wife, let her stand up and bend in a perpendicular form. She does not need any support. Hold her butt and insert your erected penis into her vagina and let the ride begin.

Flexible Pretzel Position:

This is a technical and tricky style you can try to practice with your wife. As the name sounds, you have to be sure your wife can be able to wrap herself to ensure the success of this position.

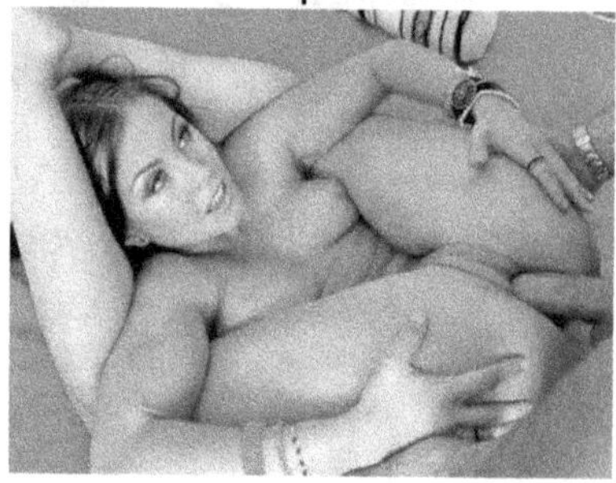

How to get started- Your wife will lay on the ground, raise her legs in such a way that it will wrap above her head with her head between her legs. She will be holding her butts as well. You will support her butt to get balance while you ride her. This very position generates the deepest penetration capable of making her scream as the intercourse is ongoing.

The Snow Angel Position:
This is a unique position that requires your wife to be in a relaxed state during intercourse.

How to get started- Let your wife lay flat on the ground. Mount on her while she spreads her legs small. Insert your penis into her pussy in the opposite direction and ride her as you maintain support with your hands.

See you in the next section!!

Chapter Nine

Techniques to Adopt for Oral Sex

To be frank with you, some couples don't like this kind of sex. Some do see it as a taboo but one man's food is another man's poison. It all boils down to choice making.

Oral sex simply means a sexual activity that involves the use of mouth, lips, and tongue to stimulate each other's genitals for sexual satisfaction as partially discussed in chapter two. This kind of sex can be done both with the anus and vagina. It is more sensual and pleasurable with a vagina, it has been recorded that about 59% of women love giving oral sex than men with 52%.

Therefore some of the Techniques to Adopt for Oral Sex are:
Blow Job:

This is the process of the female partner licking and sucking the private part of the male partner to stimulate sexual urge which will result in free ejaculation. If the two parties do not want to perform sexual intercourse properly. It is also an act to prepare the husband for sexual intercourse. It is known as cunniling.

69 Position:

This sex position has been recorded to be more vulnerable to women. However, performing this position will make your wife be highly connected with you because of the amount of vulnerability it requires. All that is required is just digging it deeply with your face positioned on her vagina or anus and allow your tongue to be at work as illustrated in the picture above. This exercise is called fellatio.

Standing O:

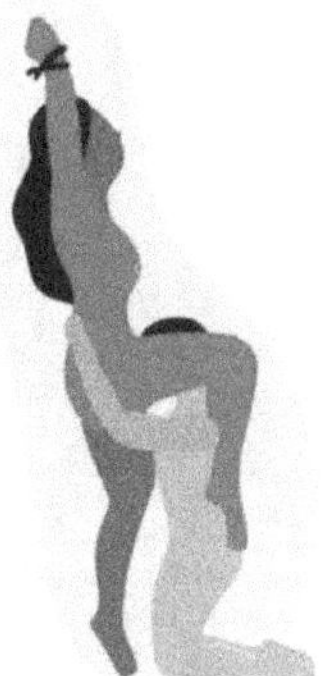

This is another oral sex position where one of the partners keeps standing, probably with his hands or her hands tied up to avoid distraction during the process. The other partner will then kneel and begin to caress, lick, and suck the private part of the other partner until a climax is reached.

What to Do Before Oral Sex

Ensure it is your wife. It is not advisable to perform oral sex especially with someone who is not your wife. This is to avoid contracting a sexually transmitted disease (STD).

Both of you should take a shower properly before engaging in oral sex. It will enable you to enjoy it to the fullest without any restrictions.

Ensure there is a mutual agreement before engaging in it to avoid having a boring moment.

See you in the next chapter as I unveil various positions you can adopt with your wife during pregnancy!!

Chapter Ten

Proven Sex Positions To Get Pregnant

In marriage, there are primary factors that are needed to have Joy and make marriage complete. One of these primary factors is **recreation**. Many marriages are in jeopardy due to this very factor.

Therefore, some of the sex positions you should practice for easy conception will be discussed here.

Furthermore, if you have been brainstorming on what to do to produce a male or female child, the solution to it is here also.

The Best Way to Calculate Your Ovulation
The very first day you begin to see your menstruation, carry out the following instructions. I will use 28 days cycle for this illustration.

Step One:
You need to count 15 days including the first day your menstrual cycle started. Ensure you get a calendar to be able to follow up on the analysis very well.

Step Two:

Indicate on the 15th day on your calendar with a marker or pen.

Step Three:

Take note of three days before the 15th day and three days after the 15th day as well.

Step Four:

From the indications you took on your calendar, you will discover it is made up of seven days. The seven days represent your ovulation days which is also fertile days. You will have about 97% chances of getting pregnant within seven days if you have sex with your partner.

Step Five:

When you practice the aforementioned steps carefully every month, you will conceive.

Note: This explanation is specifically for the period of 28days cycle. This is the reason why I counted 15 days from the first day of the period.

In case yours is not for the period stated above, below is the list of other cycles

21 days menstrual cycle is 8 days count from the first day of the bloodstain (period).

22 days menstrual cycle is 9 days count from the first day of the bloodstain.

23 days menstrual cycle is 10 days count from the first day of the bloodstain.

24 days menstrual cycle is 11 days count from the first day of the bloodstain.

25 days menstrual cycle is 12 days count from the first day of the bloodstain.

26 days menstrual cycle is 13 days count from the first day of the bloodstain.

27 days menstrual cycle is 14 days count from the first day of the bloodstain.

28 days menstrual cycle is 15 days count from the first day of the bloodstain.

29 days menstrual cycle is 16 days count from the first day of the bloodstain.

30 days menstrual cycle is 17 days count from the first day of the bloodstain.

31 days menstrual cycle is 18 days count from the first day of the bloodstain.

For instance,

If your period is 10th May, 15 days after the first day of the bloodstain will be on the 24th of May which is two weeks after counting from the 10th of May.

Three days before the 15th day are 21th, 22nd, and 23rd.

Three days after the 24th of May are 25th, 26th, and 27th.

From 21th to 27th of May which is seven days is the period of your ovulation. It is technically your fertile or conception season. Also, know that spermatozoa are always active for four days in a woman's body. So, any sexual intercourse within the period of ovulation will surely fertilize your egg.

How to Know When to Conceive a Baby Girl and a Baby Boy

This is a problematic thing for couples especially when your wife is giving birth for one gender concurrently. Well, I have got you covered with this book.

So, if you want to conceive for any gender of your choice, follow the steps below.

If you want to get pregnant for a baby girl, make love with your partner at most three days before the ovulation day.

Take note that female spermatozoa stay inside the woman's body for four days because its movement is extremely slow.

For a baby boy, make love with your partner on the very day of your ovulation and three days after the ovulation.

To make it more effective, desist from having sex with your wife for like two weeks before the week of the ovulation. It will enhance your chances of producing a baby boy.

Sex Positions To Get Pregnant

Missionary Style:
This is one of the sex styles that can adapt to get pregnant easily. The law of gravity enables the spermatozoa to flow speedily to the cervix of your wife during her ovulation period.

Doggy Style:
This is another style which we discussed earlier in the previous chapter and it is highly recommended to practice if you want to get your wife pregnant.

Legs Up Missionary:
This position is also suitable to practice if you want to get your wife pregnant.

Wheelbarrow:

This is another unique and a little technical sex position that can also well get your sperm faster into the cervix of your woman to propel conception.

Reverse Cowgirl:

This method is practiced when you are highly stimulated. It pumps the sperm into the cervix in an upward direction.

The Sensual Spoon:

Another awesome sex position that is highly recommended for pregnant women is the sensual spoon. It is an advanced level of spooning position which can be practiced from the first trimester to the last trimester.

Cowgirl Position:
Both of you can as well practice this position but you need to assist her in thrusting her waist.

These are the sex positions you should practice with your wife when she is pregnant.

See you in the next section!!

Chapter Eleven

Conclusion

One thing is to get knowledge, another thing is to implement what you have learned.

You have discovered so many ways to strategically improve your sex life in your marriage in this book. It is pertinent to as well as practice every single thing you have acquired therein.

It will be a pleasure, to get your feedback on how this book truly rekindled your sexual life. Do not also hesitate to recommend it to your friends who might be needing it as well.

Congratulations as you embark on a sexual vacation with your partner to take it to the next level.

To get updates on my publications, follow me on the author's handle.

See you in my next book!!!

www.ingramcontent.com/pod-product-compliance
Lightning Source LLC
Chambersburg PA
CBHW072125150726
47999CB00005B/2138